D0535684

HOT!
HEAT ENERGY

Emma Carlson Berne

PowerKiDS press

New York

Published in 2013 by The Rosen Publishing Group, Inc.
29 East 21st Street, New York, NY 10010

First Edition

Editor: Jennifer Way
Book Design: Andrew Povolny

Photo Credits: Cover Greg Pease/Stone/Getty Images; p. 4 Maciej Toporowicz, NYC/Flickr/Getty Images; p. 5 Ableimages/Photodisc/Thinkstock; p. 6 Digital Vision/Getty Images; pp. 7, 14, 17 Hemera/Thinkstock; p. 8 Tom Grill/Shutterstock.com; p. 9 Boyan Dimitrov/Shutterstock.com; p. 10 iStockphoto/Thinkstock; p. 11 Pixland/Thinkstock; p. 12 Image Source/Getty Images; pp. 12, 22 iStockphoto/Thinkstock; p. 13 (top) iStockphoto/Thinkstock; p. 13 (bottom) Blend Images/Shutterstock.com; p. 15 Ben Cranke/The Image Bank/Getty Images; p. 16 Jeff Randall/Photodisc/Thinkstock; pp. 18–19 Steve Bower/Shutterstock.com; p. 20 David Oxberry/Riser/Getty Images; p. 21 FloridaStock/Shutterstock.com.

Library of Congress Cataloging-in-Publication Data

Berne, Emma Carlson.
Hot! : heat energy / by Emma Carlson Berne. — 1st ed.
    p. cm. — (Energy everywhere)
Includes index.
ISBN 978-1-4488-9647-9 (library binding) — ISBN 978-1-4488-9752-0 (pbk.) — ISBN 978-1-4488-9753-7 (6-pack)
1. Heat—Juvenile literature. 2. Thermodynamics—Juvenile literature. I. Title.
QC256.B47 2013
536—dc23
                                        2012017917

Manufactured in the United States of America

CPSIA Compliance Information: Batch #W13PK4: For Further Information contact Rosen Publishing, New York, New York at 1-800-237-9932

CONTENTS

HEAT IN OUR WORLD

Energy is the ability of a system to do work. Energy comes in many forms, like light and sound. Heat is also energy. The warmth from the Sun or a stove are examples of heat energy, which is also called **thermal energy**.

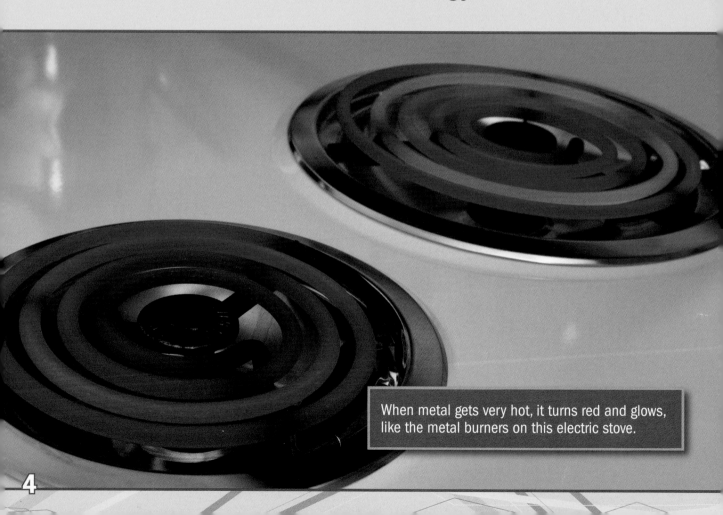

When metal gets very hot, it turns red and glows, like the metal burners on this electric stove.

Heat energy flows from objects of higher **temperature** to objects of lower temperature. An example of this is when the heat energy in a bowl of soup passes through the bowl, which you can then feel with your hands. This book is going to explain how heat energy works.

The heat of this boy's soup moves through the cup he is holding to his hands. This is an example of the movement of heat energy that happens every day.

MOVING PARTICLES

Touch your chair or desk. You are touching **matter**. Matter is anything that takes up space and has weight. A speck of dust is matter. An elephant is, too. Everything that is matter is made up of tiny bits called **particles**. The particles are constantly moving around and hitting each other. Even solid objects, like an apple, are made of moving particles.

The desk you are sitting at and the paper you write on are all made up of matter. You are made up of matter, too!

The particles in the red-hot link of this chain are moving faster than the links that are not being heated.

When particles hit each other, they create heat. The faster the particles move, the hotter the object is. The particles that make up the Sun are moving fast. The particles that make up an icicle are moving slowly.

STATES OF MATTER

Matter can exist in three ways. It can be solid, like a tree. It can be a liquid, like water. Matter can also be a **gas**, such as oxygen.

Heat and cooling can cause matter to change states. For example, think of an ice cube. An ice cube is very cold, and it is solid. Now picture the ice cube melting. It turns

Water can exist as all three states of matter. Here it is as a liquid drop of rain.

The water in this iron is heated until it turns into steam. As the water transforms from liquid into gas, it is used to smooth the wrinkles out of clothes.

into water, which is a liquid. Now put that water into a teakettle, and heat it up even more. What comes out of the spout? That same water has been transformed into steam, a gas.

SOURCES OF HEAT ENERGY

The giant, flaming Sun is one of the biggest sources of heat energy. Any kind of fire, though, such as a campfire, a candle flame, or the gas flame on a stove burner, is also heat energy.

The Sun is a source of heat energy to Earth. That is why it is usually warmer during the day than at night.

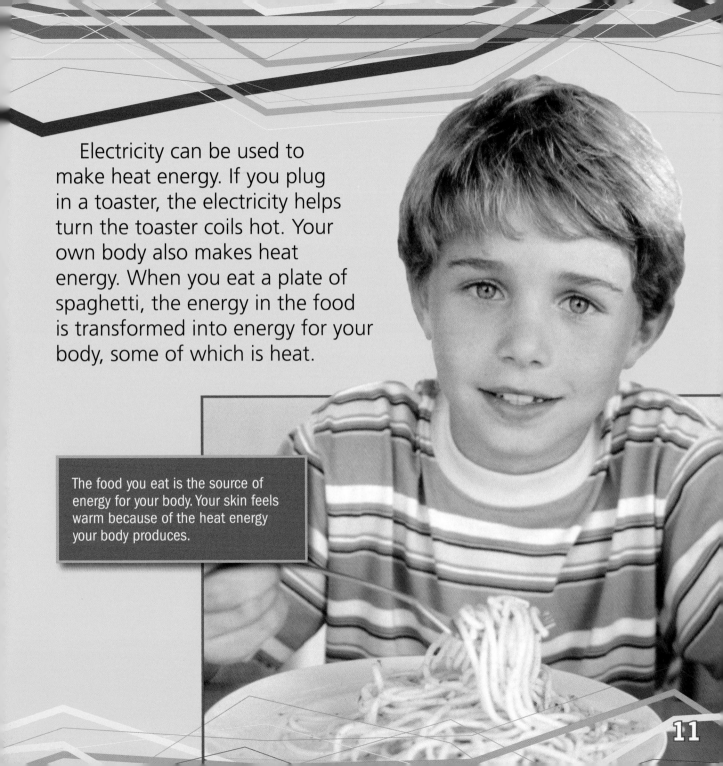

Electricity can be used to make heat energy. If you plug in a toaster, the electricity helps turn the toaster coils hot. Your own body also makes heat energy. When you eat a plate of spaghetti, the energy in the food is transformed into energy for your body, some of which is heat.

The food you eat is the source of energy for your body. Your skin feels warm because of the heat energy your body produces.

HEAT IN YOUR HOME

If you walk through your house, you will find different examples of heat. See that pot of soup boiling on the stove in the kitchen? Then, in the living room, your mother has lit a candle. The lightbulb in that lamp is also a source of heat. The hair dryer in the bathroom gets hot very quickly when it is plugged in.

Heat energy is used for cooking. Ovens and stoves are sources of heat in the kitchen.

A radiator is a common source of heat in homes.

In the backyard, the Sun has warmed the towels on the clothesline. What about the asphalt driveway on a sunny summer day? The Sun's heat has made it too hot to walk on barefoot!

When you hang laundry on the clothesline, the Sun's heat energy is used to dry it.

HEAT IN EARTH

Our planet is a naturally hot place. Inside the center of Earth, different substances are breaking down. As they break down, they release a lot of heat. Some of this heat makes its way to the surface of Earth. Volcanoes are a great example of heat energy from Earth. When volcanoes erupt, they spew hot liquid rock and gases.

Heat energy also comes from Earth in the form of hot springs. Water that is heated within Earth flows from natural openings in Earth's surface. People all around the world enjoy bathing and swimming in hot springs.

The inside of Earth is so hot that rock is liquid. When liquid rock, or lava, comes out of a volcano, it becomes solid rock as it cools.

WHY ARE HOT SPRINGS HOT?

The water in hot springs is heated naturally under the surface of Earth. Sometimes this is because the water is near a volcano. The water finds a crack in Earth's crust and bubbles out, already hot!

These monkeys are relaxing in a hot spring in Japan. This water is comfortable for the monkeys even though it is the middle of winter!

WAYS TO MEASURE HEAT ENERGY

When you are sick, your parents might use a thermometer to check your body's temperature. A thermometer is a tool that measures how much heat energy is released from something. You might also see thermometers outside people's houses, to measure how hot or cold the air temperature is.

When you are sick, your parent may use a thermometer to take your temperature. You have a fever if your temperature is higher than about 98.6° F (37° C).

This thermometer shows temperature measurements in both Celsius and Fahrenheit.

Thermometers measure temperature in **degrees**. Fahrenheit and Celsius are the two major systems of measurement. In the United States, we measure temperature in Fahrenheit. With this measurement, your body's temperature should be 98.6 degrees. Most countries use Celsius. In Celsius degrees, your body's temperature would measure 37 degrees.

WHAT ARE BTUS?

"BTU" stands for "British thermal unit." It is another way of measuring heat. One BTU is the amount of energy needed to heat up 1 pound (454 g) of water so it gets 1° F (.6° C) hotter.

HEAT ENERGY ON THE MOVE

Thermal energy does not just stay in one place. In fact, it is always shifting and flowing from one place to another. Heat is the result of the movement of thermal energy from one object to another. This movement is called **heat transfer**.

Thermal energy is always flowing from hotter to cooler objects. For example, if you were to lie down on a cool tile floor, the tile beneath your body would become warm. Some of the heat from your body transferred to the cool floor.

In a hot-air balloon, the burner heats the air in the balloon. As the warm air moves toward cooler air, it lifts the balloon into the sky.

CHANGING HEAT ENERGY

Heat energy can also be converted, or changed into other useful forms. For instance, a steam train's engine converts heat energy into mechanical energy. The engine burns coal and transforms that heat into steam, and the steam powers the engine. Your parents' car runs by converting heat energy to mechanical energy also. The moving parts inside the engine rub against each other, creating **friction**. The friction releases heat energy.

When you make toast, electricity is converted to heat energy. The heating coils in the toaster let off heat as well as light.

This steam engine can convert heat energy into mechanical energy, but it cannot create or destroy energy.

Even if energy is converted, though, the amount of energy that exists always stays the same. Energy cannot be created or destroyed. All the energy in our world gets converted over and over.

PROTECTING ENERGY RESOURCES

Energy comes from many sources. For example, **geothermal energy** is the heat energy inside the Earth. It can be used to make electricity. Coal is an energy source that comes from inside the Earth, too. Coal will eventually run out because it is a **nonrenewable** energy source.

Renewable sources, like geothermal, wind, and **solar energy**, can never be used up. It is up to us not to waste the nonrenewable sources we use to power our world.

Wind is a renewable source of energy. These wind turbines collect the wind's energy and convert it to electricity.

GLOSSARY

degrees (dih-GREEZ) A measurement of how hot or cold something is.

friction (FRIK-shin) The rubbing of one thing against another.

gas (GAS) A fluid, like water or air, with no solid shape.

geothermal energy (JEE-oh-ther-mul EH-ner-jee) The heat energy stored in the Earth.

heat transfer (HEET TRANS-fer) Passing heat from one place or object to another.

matter (MA-ter) Anything that has weight and takes up space.

nonrenewable (non-ree-NOO-uh-bul) Not able to be replaced once used.

particles (PAR-tih-kulz) Small pieces of matter.

renewable (ree-NOO-uh-bul) Able to be replaced once it is used up.

solar energy (SOH-ler EH-nur-jee) Heat and light created by the Sun.

temperature (TEM-pur-cher) How hot or cold something is.

thermal energy (THER-mul EH-nur-jee) Energy from heat.

INDEX

F
form(s), 4, 14, 20
friction, 20

G
gas(es), 8–9, 14, 22

H
heat transfer, 18

I
icicle, 7

L
light, 4
liquid, 8–9

M
matter, 6, 8

O
oxygen, 8

P
particles, 6–7

S
sound, 4
steam, 9, 20
stove, 4, 12
Sun, 4, 7, 10, 13, 22
system(s), 4, 17

T
temperature, 5, 16–17
thermometer(s), 16–17

WEBSITES

Due to the changing nature of Internet links, PowerKids Press has developed an online list of websites related to the subject of this book. This site is updated regularly. Please use this link to access the list: www.powerkidslinks.com/enev/hot/